PATHWAYS THROUGH DEPRESSION

*This book is dedicated to all the caring people
I have met through Depression Alliance,
especially my lovely friend Maggy.*

Pathways
through
depression

SUE ATKINSON

A LION BOOK

A Lion Book
an imprint of
Lion Hudson plc
Mayfield House, 256 Banbury Road,
Oxford OX2 7DH, England
www.lionhudson.com
ISBN 0 7459 5137 6

First edition 2004
10 9 8 7 6 5 4 3 2 1 0

Acknowledgments

Cover image: Digital Vision.
Pictures on pp. 3 Digital Vision, 10–11 Jessica Aidley,
12 Prospero/Alamy, 20–21 Nick Rous, 22–23 Image100/Alamy,
29 Nick Rous, 30 Lion Hudson/David Townsend,
37 Image State/Alamy, 38–39 Christopher Gomersall/Alamy,
45 Digital Vision, 46 Rod Edwards/Alamy.

A catalogue record for this book is available
from the British Library

Typeset in 10.5/12.5 Goudy Old Style BT
Printed and bound in China

CONTENTS

INTRODUCTION

Depression is the worst pain known to humans.
A DOCTOR AT A CONFERENCE ABOUT DEPRESSION

This book is for depressed people who are

* looking for a pathway through depression, stress and burnout

* trying to find inner peace

* trying to get in touch with their inner spirit

Depression is an utterly awful illness. It isn't just feeling a bit low. It is a potentially life-threatening illness and we can feel

* despair and worthlessness

* guilt and shame

* appalling loneliness

* so sad that we cry frequently

* so anxious, stressed and fearful that normal life is impossible

* unable to concentrate

* a sense that we don't 'fit in'

- uninterested in everything around us

- we are so useless that there is no point going on with life

- as if God and everyone else have abandoned us

- life seems not to be worth living

HOW TO USE THIS BOOK

It is often hard to concentrate when we are depressed, so the text is broken up to make it easy to read. You can dip into the book anywhere and just read what you can cope with today.

I've linked our journey out of depression to the four seasons. Many of us feel much worse in winter and need more daylight to feel better. It can be that turning to the natural world around us we can find some sense of peace, seeing our depression as a part of the ups and downs of life, just like the four seasons.

Each of the four sections has four main headings.

What we need to know

Under this heading are things that we need to understand about depression if we are to be able to manage it well enough to get back to some kind of 'normal' life, such as:

- The depression will go away one day! It's

important to cling onto that fact.

🌱 For some people, the depression never comes back.

Thoughts along the way

These are some of the issues we need to think about if we are to find a pathway out of depression, such as

🌱 learning to deal with our anger

🌱 working out what forgiveness might mean

Pathways through depression

Each chapter has a section with ideas that can help us to get out of depression, such as learning to deal with hopeless advice and inane platitudes!

🌱 'Pray about it and you will get better' is advice that probably means well but often just increases guilt. Many of us need medication to get our brain chemistry in balance. However, prayer and meditation can be hugely important in our struggle back to health.

🌱 Those who think we just need to 'pull ourselves together' have no idea how far the devastation of depression is from the ordinary experience of 'feeling low'.

Finding our pathway out of depression can take

surprising turns. I found that

- laughing at funny television programmes or doing vigorous exercise results in positive feelings
- it is crucial to find a creative way to get depression 'out there' where I can see it, instead of seeing it as a part of my inner world

Meditations

Meditating is a very reassuring thing. It can

- help us to 'come out' from within ourselves and feel more in touch with the world around us
- lower our blood pressure and stress levels
- help us to find our inner strength

Meditating is also a way of communicating with God. The God of Abraham, the God of Handel's *Messiah*, the one some call the Ground of Our Being or Great Creator, is what is in my head with the word 'God' for me. But you might mean 'Love' or something quite different.

Our thoughts about God are often words, but our communications with our Creator can be in any form. I use words in this book alongside photos, but you can try to get beyond the words and let the photos speak to your mind.

Instead of words you might want to think of images, or do a painting or just let yourself relax in the presence of God. You don't need to *say* anything.

If there is a difference between me and my friends,
it's that I'm on a spiritual passage and they are not.
MADONNA

Here are some meditations to help you begin your pathway through depression.

DAWN

When we see the glory of the sun setting, we sit awhile to take it in.

It can be a time of fear – how will I face the darkness?

It can be a time of rest and refreshment – but how will I get everything done that I have to do?

It can be a time of some certainty and hope.

- ❧ We believe that in the morning the sun will rise again.
- ❧ We wait in hope for the dawn.

We can be reasonably certain that there will be a dawn! That belief in dawn can help us as we search for a pathway, because we can see that it is part of the way that the world is made. There are times of darkness and fear, but these are followed by times of light when we can see more clearly and get on with our lives again.

FINDING SOME MEANING THROUGH PAIN

The way ahead can seem long and bleak.

Our pain can be so difficult to deal with that we wonder if it is worth going on.

One of the most crucial questions we need to

ask ourselves as we try to find a way out of our depression is: which way are we heading?

- 🌱 Are we heading towards a life of recriminations and bitterness, or towards love and forgiveness?
- 🌱 Are we being destructive in our relationships or being a creative peacemaker?

As well as being a place of beauty, the world is also a place of hurt, anger and destruction. It can feel excruciatingly awful!

If we love at all we are likely to get hurt – maybe inevitably hurt. But would we want the world to be a love-free zone? Maybe that would make an even worse world!

So perhaps feeling depressed is an appropriate response to our world. None of us can escape pain.

We even need some kinds of pain. For example, a child must learn that fire hurts and that deep water can be dangerous. The pain we experience in depression can be like that – something to learn from.

Sorrow… may sadden your face, but it sharpens your understanding.
FROM ECCLESIASTES 7

My God, why…?
JESUS OF NAZARETH

WINTER
At a low point

From the ends of the earth I call to you as my heart grows weary. Lead me to the rock that is higher and stronger than I am.
FROM PSALM 61

What we need to know

We can become depressed for many different reasons.

We lose something important to us.

- We are separated from a loved one through death or desertion.

- We get older and lose our youthful energy, looks and maybe our health. Our body refuses to do what it used to do.

- We lose our self-esteem in some way – we lose our job, we don't get the promotion we thought we would get, we can't get employment because of our depression or something else happens that makes us feel useless and worthless.

- We lose our confidence if we work too hard and have burnout, relationships change and there are many things about life that we do not understand and do not like, such as working for a tyrannical boss.

- ❧ We move house and lose our security or a friend.

- ❧ We lose our strength through illness or accident. For example, flu can cause changes in our body, as can the loss of good bacteria in our gut after taking antibiotics.

- ❧ We find that we have lost our faith in God.

In other words, something happens that means we lose our inner peace and feel so rattled that ordinary life cannot go on. Even losing a precious object can be the trigger that starts the depressing thoughts.

We find life tough.

- ❧ Having a baby turns out to be harder than we thought and our hormones are all over the place.

- ❧ Memories get triggered. It seems that children who have to face situations too hard for them to cope with can bury their feelings deeply within themselves. But later on in life, if something happens that awakens those pent-up feelings, that inner rage, fear and confusion can emerge as depression or phobias, or thoughts that now keep popping out at them unexpectedly and intrusively.

🌹 It is very common for people to develop depression as a response to their childhood. This depression can start in teenage years or even earlier, but often it comes when we are adults. We are not helped when people say to us, 'But that was long ago – get over it.' We try to, but it can take us years.

As a result of all this our body can get out of balance and depression hits.

Some people do not understand depression and they see it as something shameful. Some are prejudiced towards people with mental health problems. This can make us resentful and angry, and we might try to hide our depression rather than seeking help – especially if the help on offer is based on ignorance.

There are no quick fixes with depression!

Thoughts along the way

Depression can tend to make us lose interest in creative things we used to enjoy doing, such as cooking, gardening and reading. But this loss of our relaxing and creative side can pull us downwards into more depression. It is hard in the depths of depression to want to do *anything*, but we need to give ourselves time to be creative and enjoy our hobbies.

Pathways through depression

❧ **Asking for help**
If our body chemistry is out of balance, medication can help to get us back in balance again. Doctors have found that during some forms of depression there are not enough of some chemicals in the brain, such as serotonin. Taking tablets can help put that right.

Some kind of 'talking therapy' can help us, especially when we have begun to stabilize through taking antidepressants for a while.

❧ **Finding out more about our inner life**
We find that although depression is utterly awful, the much more horrific thing is what is behind our depression. What is it that we cannot face? We will almost certainly need some kind of help to find that out.

❧ **Learning to manage our anger**
During times of depression many people find they are furiously angry inside. Some people even believe that much depression is about suppressed anger. However, for others, in deep depression they can't feel anything. But as they move along the road

towards healing, their anger might begin to show.

❧ Shaking our fist at God
When we see our anger, we are seeing one of
the most important pathways out of depression.
Let yourself rage and spit venom! Just don't do
something aggressive to someone else!

❧ Hope not despair
One of the hardest pathways out of depression
is turning utter despair into something more
hopeful. Despair is powerful stuff, and it is crucial
that we gradually search out pathways that are
more hopeful – such as reading this book.

Our depression will end! We might not feel
that it will – but it will!

❧ The gift of tears
For most of us, eventually, tears are crucial to
helping us find a way out of depression. They
are a way of expressing our feelings, and everyone
needs to do that.

Some people believe that depression can be
about suppressed feelings and the horrible 'big
boys don't cry' stuff that we hear parents saying
to their sons.

Everyone needs to cry. Tears are healing. They
are positive – they can teach us the depth of our
feelings and show us that we must not go on
ignoring our emotions.

❧ Focusing on positive images

Depression is hard enough without surrounding ourselves with negative or critical people or images!

Watch out for things like the power of television constantly giving us bad news – it can reinforce our sense of despair and feed into our nightmares.

❧ Making a special box

One of the ways I've found a pathway through depression is to make a special box (or book) and put things into it on my better days, or when someone sends me something that helps me to feel I'm on a pathway out of depression.

My box is covered in my favourite fabric, but you could just use an old shoe box and cover it in gift-wrap paper.

My box has cards, photos and objects inside that remind me how much I am loved and how much I love others.

But also, there is space inside my box, just as there is space inside me.

And in that space, God is.

God is in all of us, the 'ground of our being', and it is finding that spiritual core in us that teaches us how to meditate – just being quiet and knowing

God is there,
    holding us,
    loving us,
    leading us.

Meditation isn't some trick – something clever.
It is simply being aware of the spiritual core of
our life, God in us, strengthening us.
    So when I look in my special box
(on bad days when I need some
comfort), I see the space inside it,
and it reminds me of the God-space
inside me, and I can touch that deep
place within myself.

Meditations

THE CYCLES OF LIFE

Trees look dead in winter, but inside
there is still a bit of life, though it is
well hidden.
    The death that winter brings is a
time of rest. We wait and hope for the
new life of spring.

Depression can be a time to rest,
to look at our life in a different way,
to learn what it is that caused us to

plunge into depression in the first place.

We can learn to see our depression as a time of darkness that is a natural part of the cycles of life – rest, renewal, abundant life and dying down.

We have to try to cling on to hope. To give up on it is to deny that the world is made the way it is, with all its cycles.

WHAT DO WE REALLY WANT OUT OF LIFE?

Our world is a confusing place, and it is all too easy to lose our way. Finding the right track can be difficult and can take considerable time.

Sometimes we go the wrong way and have to come back to the start.

Making decisions during depression can be difficult. We need to ask ourselves what is really crucial and important about life.

Is it money?

A good job?

Having expensive holidays, or a car or a big house?

Or is it about being happy, doing things we enjoy and helping others along the way?

What if we only had another month to live? What would we do today?

What do we really want out of life?

For the master spirit of the earth shall not sleep peacefully upon the wind till the needs of the least of you are satisfied.
KAHLIL GIBRAN

SPRING

Signs of growth

When we have accepted the worst, we have nothing more to lose. And that automatically means we have everything to gain.

DALE CARNEGIE

What we need to know

- All humans need love and affection, and during depression we seem to need more emotional support than ever. However, it can seem harder to receive this support and we can feel that those around us are not able or willing to give us the support that we need.

- It is very hard for our carers. Sometimes they can feel that whatever they do to help us, we interpret it as no help at all!

- It is crucial that we have someone we can talk to. This is where depression charities such as Depression Alliance can help. Even if we feel deserted by friends and family, we can become part of a self-help group (an actual group that meets or an online group).

- Our internal voice might be telling us things

24

we don't really want to hear.

You're a terrible and worthless person.

You don't deserve a place on God's earth.

Life will never be any different for you.

You are so angry you might damage someone, so you had better do lots of good things to make up for being so wicked.

Thoughts along the way

If we don't take notice of our inner life and feelings, they will cause nothing but trouble as they demand attention.

Maybe we talk too little to each other about our inner lives, as if they were some kind of secret that we cannot share – almost as if it were wicked to have an inner life.

But my inner life is full of images, feelings, dreams, fantasies, stories that I make up and live, people who I love and talk to, and comforting words and thoughts that I let myself dwell on to soothe pain or to reassure myself.

We need to feed this positive side of our imagination, reflecting on what is good and joyful – keeping our mind on where we want to be in a year's time. But as we let our thoughts soar, we must be aware of the darker side of our imagination and learn to turn from that back to what makes us feel 'good'.

I'm sure some people might regard this imaginative inner world as an escape or denial of reality. It probably is, but, along with the 'masks' we can wear to hide our real feelings, I think that having strategies to escape from the awfulness of the 'real' world around us is a crucial part of surviving depression!

Little by little you will learn to distinguish between the ways of peace and light and the ways of darkness.
JEAN VANIER

Pathways through depression

❦ Searching for inner peace
Learning to listen to our inner world is to learn to live at peace with ourselves.

Our unexplained panic attacks and feelings of deep fear have their root in something – and by talking to someone, writing, painting or doing something else creative, we can learn to understand our panic and work towards a place of greater inner peace.

❦ Caring for our physical body
We tend to neglect ourselves during depression. To feel better we need to get back to healthy eating, a brisk walk every day and taking medical advice about developing regular sleep patterns.

❧ Freedom to choose

We have a glorious yet awesome freedom to choose what we do with our lives. We can get bogged down in negative things that trap us in anger or hate or bitterness. Or we can choose to think creatively and replace hate and bitterness with forgiveness, and this will make us feel better.

❧ Forgiveness

We can feel horribly pushed into being told we 'must forgive'. This can become an enormous pressure on us.

Forgiving is hard! It can take a long time. Some of the hurts of childhood, for example, are very difficult to forgive, especially when the person who hurt us shows absolutely no remorse whatsoever.

But if we can gradually 'let go' of our anger and resentment, it can have a positive effect on our well-being.

❧ Our unique creativity

Our creativity is unique to us. No one else will write that poem or make those shelves the way we would do it.

If you don't do it, the world will never see it and will be the poorer for that – whatever your negative thinking is telling you!

So get gardening, making music, dancing,

producing a community newspaper, running the after-school club and teaching children to make rockets out of washing-up liquid bottles.

❧ Using the 'good enough' principle
Depressed people can tend towards perfectionism. But that can trap us in depression.

One of the most important ways through depression can be to learn to be 'good enough'.

Whenever you beat yourself up about something and tell yourself you are a hopeless and worthless human being, try saying 'OK, I'm not the best (parent, cook, driver, carer of my elderly relative or whatever), but I'm good enough.'

When we forgive we ride the crest of love's cosmic wave; we walk in stride with God. And we heal the hurt we never deserved.
LEWIS SMEDES

Meditations

BETTER THINGS ARE TO COME
If we search out the God of creation, we may find we encounter God-thoughts in small things.

We see the first daring snowdrops of spring, when we seem to have had winter for so long and the ground is frozen. We look at them, amazed at their beauty and at their courage and strength to push up through the bitterly hard earth when nothing else will dare to flower.

The message they bring each year is so special.

They speak of the end of the bleakest of winters.

They tell us that we need to go on hoping for an end to the sadness and alienation of depression.

Better things are to come.

Living in the northern hemisphere, spring is also when I think of Easter and, along with Easter bunnies and chicks, of new life and resurrection.

I am the resurrection and the life.
JESUS OF NAZARETH

DEATH IS FOLLOWED BY NEW LIFE

Plants have their times of growth and flowering.
Then the seeds are pollinated and they fall, going
their own way in the world to become a new plant.

Seeds can usually survive a long time after they
fall. They are at rest, sleeping through the toughness
of winter, when conditions are too difficult for them
to grow well.

But for the seed to grow into a new plant, the
seed itself will have to die. There can be no new life
except through this process of death.

*If Jesus the healer taught us anything, he taught us
that the way to salvation lies through vulnerability.*
M. SCOTT PECK

SUMMER

Transformation and creativity

*Stop telling God how big your storm is. Instead,
tell your storm how big your God is.*

FROM AN ANONYMOUS EMAIL

What we need to know

It can be very difficult for a depressed person to be realistic.

❧ We need to keep reminding ourselves that depression does come to an end.

❧ No one can wave a magic wand and get rid of the feelings for us.

If, like me, you have 'high' manic phases, we need to learn to keep in touch with reality during those times. That's tough, because these 'highs' can be such a relief after the gloom that it is all too easy to get carried away. So beware!

❧ 'Highs' can be the times when we feel most creative and full of such joy and wonder at the universe. So if we can use these times in some positive way, they can help us find the pathways through depression.

31

- Many creative people do their best work both during times of deepest depression and also when they feel 'high'.

We need to use our good days to

- laugh as much as we can!

- prepare for the harder days – perhaps writing how a good day feels and putting that where we will see it on a bad day

We can do something like

- fly a kite

- go to the children's library for a few hours and sit and read children's books

- share with someone the enjoyment of a chocolate brownie or a brilliant novel

- go out with our mates and do something silly like bungee jumping

Thoughts along the way

There are so many things about our world that don't make sense. We seem to be more acutely aware of this when we feel depressed.

Innocent people get caught up in wars, and children suffer in ways that make us think that

God cannot possibly be a God of love.

Volcanoes, tidal waves, storms, floods, tornadoes and icebergs are all natural things that we have no control over. That may worry us because we wonder why a Great Creator who can make beautiful things like a swallow-tailed butterfly and a baby deer should have made a world like that.

For me it is a greater leap of faith to believe that our world came about through some random accident than to believe that it is the work of a talented creator – albeit that it seems left in a half-finished unstable state!

So God has given the natural world its own freedom to be what it is. The world has freedom and we have freedom.

Suffering is ultimately a mystery.
RUSSELL STANNARD, BRITISH SCIENTIST

Pathways through depression

❧ Forgiving can be a long process

We are likely to need to go on working at forgiving others and ourselves. We all want justice when we have been wronged, and rightly so, but sometimes we have to 'let go' of our hurts in order to find a place of peace. We won't always get an apology. We won't always get justice. But if we 'let go' and turn our back on bitterness, we will find peace, and this will contribute hugely to the quality of our lives.

❧ Searching for inner joy

We need to find out more about what makes us feel 'on top' and creative, and what it is that gives us inner joy. This might sound a bit grand, but I've found that growing vegetables (even just cress on a window sill) fills me with delight. Seeing those little green bits peeping up through the soil gives my inner world a great boost.

❧ Transformation

Depression is hell on earth, and we rightly rage at God about why we have to suffer it. But if we can in some way use our depression as a way of starting to transform our lives and the lives of those around us, we will be doing something purely creative that will make our hearts sing.

Once we have begun to crawl out of the hideous lonely pit, we could make some effort to

- ☙ do something for someone else, such as work in a charity shop for a day a week, or visit elderly people in a local home

- ☙ find creative things to do, such as joining an evening class

- ☙ go to a self-help group and share experiences

This transforming isn't some grand unreachable thing. It is in

- ☙ the ordinariness of our daily encounters with those around us

- ☙ the beauty of a sunset through which we connect back with our inner selves and with our Great Creator

This process of transformation will, of course, last the whole of the rest of our lives.

It is one of the fundamental contributions of pain to make people wake up to a deeper quality of existence.
MARTIN ISRAEL

Meditations

COMING THROUGH THE STORM

Watching lightning can be a terrifying experience. Listening to the thunder coming closer and closer and feeling the ground tremble can make us afraid of that one big crash just above.

Yet there is also something beautiful about the storm. The lightning mesmerizes us – we are curious about how it happens and amazed at the power of it.

Then there is the calm after the storm – when the electrical charges in the clouds are more in balance with each other, the world is more at peace with itself, and the sun comes out.

Lightning strikes the most vulnerable thing. In a family, or any other kind of group of people, sometimes the most vulnerable or susceptible person can be a 'lightning conductor'.

We pick up the stresses, strains and anger of the group and we feel the full strength of the emotion within ourselves. This can be horribly uncomfortable and the build-up of emotion (guilt, shame, etc), much of which belongs to other people, can lead to depression.

There is a sense in which we need storms in our lives – when our inner lives are out of balance and there needs to be a discharge of pent-up energy and emotions.

Somehow we bury feelings so deeply within ourselves that we don't have much conscious awareness of them – but they are creating chaos inside us!

We need to have the 'storm' to get those feelings in balance so that we can gradually become at peace with ourselves.

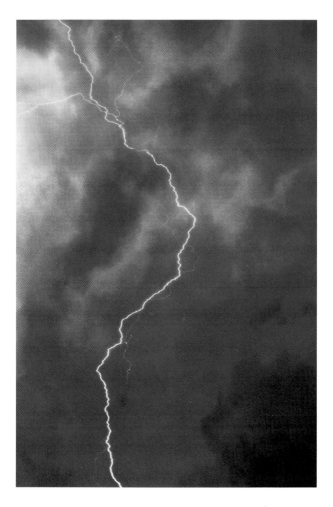

Savour the moment

When we look at a sunset, or the rain on a rose petal, or snow on a mountain or glow-worms at night, we can get an overwhelming sense of beauty.

When we go birdwatching in Scotland and there are puffins, everyone looks at these wonderful little birds and smiles. They are so stunning, so comical as they crash-land with their beaks full of sand eels, so endearing as they stand amongst the sea pinks, that we cannot fail to be amazed at them. Maybe

they are proof that God has a sense of humour!

When we see something beautiful, we can stop and savour that moment. Life can be such a rush that we forget to take time to look at creation and enjoy it, wonder at it and let ourselves be astonished by it.

I've come to earth so that you will have abundant life.
JESUS OF NAZARETH

AUTUMN
Making plans

It is amazingly empowering to have the support of a strong, motivated and inspirational group of people.
SUSAN JEFFERS

What we need to know

Finding a pathway out of depression can be a long hard slog – but we *will find a way out of it*!

Yes, there will be bad days, but if we make the most of the good days we can feel a new strength and energy for life.

- We can try out different things.

- We can work at the things that dragged us down in the first place.

- We can be bold and push ourselves a bit – maybe building into our week time for a self-help group.

- We can learn to recognize what for us triggers depressed feelings.

- It is important to be kind to ourselves and to think of several ways of doing that, such as having relaxation times or times when we can do what we *want* to do, not what we *have* to do.

We can learn to recognize our early symptoms of depression returning, such as disturbed sleep or bursting into tears.

- 🐾 We can plan what we will do if we see ourselves losing our way again.

- 🐾 We can tell ourselves we are able to handle it all because now we are wiser and know what to expect.

We can think of this as making a survival backpack in case the way ahead gets difficult again.

- 🐾 We need to make a list of people or organizations that we can ring if life gets to be too much again, such as other members of our self-help group, including online friends. Sometimes just a chat with someone can show us that the depression is controllable and that there is no way we are going to let it overwhelm us.

- 🐾 We need to make a plan with our carers about what it is that they can do to help: bring a cup of tea, give lots of hugs, don't keep on asking questions, etc.

- 🐾 If you don't have a special box (or book – see 'Winter'), this might be the time to gather together some cards, photos or poems that you value.

Thoughts along the way

Times of depression can be when we mature quickly and learn a great deal.

- ❧ We understand more about human pain.

- ❧ We learn what it means to support someone who is hurting, and we have the privilege of giving a soft touch of reassurance.

- ❧ We appreciate small things like the smile at the shop checkout and the call of an owl at night.

Our determination to make some use of the awfulness of our depression can help us to connect with others and with our Creator. We use our painful experiences and work at developing that transformation of the pain into an ability to spread love, joy and peace. This is the creative thing to do with our pain. We are making the pathway ahead clearer for others as well as ourselves.

Then we find, to our surprise, that doing something for others makes us feel better!

The greatest gift we can give each other is our own woundedness.
M. SCOTT PECK

Pathways through depression

❦ Reaching out

Once we are through the really awful bits and on a pathway to something more positive, we can work at reaching out to others and moving towards learning to trust others. This is desperately difficult for some – but unless we learn to trust a bit, we are likely to go on wandering, lost in the awful desolation that depression can bring.

If we set out to help and love those around us, we find that we are helped and loved.

If we have been hurt before and find trusting hard, it is in taking the risk of developing relationships that we find the strength to let ourselves trust.

Only by risking ourselves can we encounter another person in depth and form a strong relationship.

❦ Reflecting on what we are learning

It can be all too easy to want to forget our times of depression, but if we note down some of our insights and talk them through with a friend, we can gain a great deal of self-understanding.

Without the experience of depression we might muddle along somehow with our obsessions bugging us, our nightmares still haunting us, family problems dragging us down and with a sense that we really don't matter as a human being.

While the depression isn't at all 'good', it is an opportunity to change things for the better and find a pathway towards managing our lives positively.

We don't just suffer the depression – we use it. And that can be so empowering!

We stop seeing ourselves as worthless insignificant creatures.

We learn to be ourselves, secure in our knowledge of our place in the universe, and growing in confidence about the small but creative part we can play.

Meditations

ASTONISHING WORKS OF ART

Trees are some of the most remarkable things on our planet.

They play an important role in the way the atmosphere is balanced, changing carbon dioxide in the air into oxygen so that we can go on breathing. The annual rings in their trunks give us a picture of climate change through the centuries. Trees give us shelter and stand out in the landscape like nothing else on earth.

They are, quite simply, astonishing works of art of a creative God who gives us good things.

Trees show us one of the greatest truths of life

on earth – that death and new life are part of what makes the earth work. The acorn falls from the oak tree, but it has to die in order to grow into a new tree. In this world we cannot have new life without first having death.

We need to face the reality that the cold and death of winter are coming. It might be a long and difficult slog to get through it. But at the end there will be new life. We wouldn't appreciate the wonders of spring if it weren't for the bleakness of winter.

THE POWER OF LOVE

In all the devastation of depression and through the trials of life, there is one thing that goes on and on despite everything.

That is love.

I like the image of God as the Mother Hen –
she gathers me under her wing and protects me
like a little chick.

I can run to her when life gets tough.

I am safe.

We are 'held' by our Maker, secure, completely safe,
and loved so much that there is no way that our
earthly understanding can take it in.

We are nestling there, and the more that we let
ourselves just sit quietly and let the love surround us,
the more we will 'grow' as people and experience
that 'love that will not let us go'.

I trace the rainbow through the rain,
And feel the promise is not vain
That morn shall tearless be.
GEORGE MATHESON

We are not alone in our struggle. If we reach out
to find love, we will find it.

RESOURCES

Depression Alliance is the leading UK charity for people with depression. They

- coordinate a national network of self-help groups, including online contacts

- produce a series of free publications which offer information about depression

- publish a member-led magazine called *A Single Step* with hints and information about surviving depression and how to get help

- have offices in England, Wales and Scotland

Depression Alliance
35 Westminster Bridge Road
London
SE1 7JB
Tel: 020 7633 0557
Fax: 020 7633 0559
Email: information@depressionalliance.org
Web: www.depressionalliance.org